PAINTING SH ON THE TILTING HORIZON

Poems by

EMIL RADO

TARANIS
Books

Second Edition 1993
Published by Taranis Books

design - mason

Printed in Scotland by Clydeside Press, Glasgow

ISBN 1-873899-45-9

Some of the poems in this volume have previously appeared in *The Friend, The Herald, Lines Review, Northlight* and *Outposts*.

Contents

I have become indebted to many friends on my journey as an apprentice poet. I have gained from the criticism and the encouragement of my fellow writers in the School of Poets at the Scottish Poetry Library, Edinburgh (and Tessa Ransford in particular). I am also grateful to the many friends who have found time to comment on drafts of my poems, notably Ann Karkalas, Linna Monteath, Diane Bowes, and my wife Anne.

Emil Rado

Emil Rado was born in Hungary in 1931. He was fortunate to survive the extermination of Hungarian Jews during the war, when most of his family perished. He came to Britain in 1947 and completed his education at Ackworth, a Quaker school in Yorkshire, and at University College London.

He spent fifteen years as a lecturer in universities in Ghana, Uganda and Kenya, and a year as a visiting professor in Williams College, Massachusetts. In 1965 he joined Glasgow University, where he is a Senior Lecturer in the Department of Adult & Continuing Education.

He started writing poems in1988, mostly in English. He also writes poems in Hungarian (some of which have been broadcast on Hungarian radio), and occasional twin-poems that come to him more or less simultaneously in both languages. Three of these appear in this volume. All the poems were written between 1988 and 1992 and are printed in the order in which they were written.

His themes are the eternal ones of love and death, the joys and sorrows of friendship, and nature caught unawares. Many of his poems reflect a lifelong love-affair with the mountains and shores of Scotland, which is now his true home.

INTRODUCTION *by* ARNOLD KEMP

In his gloomier moments, the modern newspaper editor can surrender to depression about the general decline of literacy. The video and satellite dish spread inexorably through society. The publishing trade is in almost universal recession. There are lots of bookshops, but often there are more browsers than buyers. And who buys poetry any more?

Every so often an Emil Rado appears to dispel the gloom. Emil is an extremely active teacher at Glasgow University, and paid The Herald a great compliment by organising a seminar as part of his work in adult education. We were greatly cheered by the positive response from the many people who attended it. Public speaking is a bit of an ordeal, mitigated only by an audience that is attentive and interested. Thanks to Emil, all of us found our day at the University stimulating and rewarding. Perhaps there is hope for the printed press, given the public interest in this event, we reflected.

Partly as a result of that association, Emil sent us some of his poems. He started writing poetry only four years ago, mostly in English, but also in his native Hungarian. I found them both moving and accessible, and we published some of them around Christmas last year. They were well received. Perhaps, I thought, my gloom about the philistinism of the age is unjustified. Maybe there is hope for poetry, too.

Emil's poems are both universal and personal. They are universal in that they reflect and celebrate the natural world which we all share. They are universal in that their themes, of evanescence, death and reconciliation, are inescapably part both of the natural order and of the human condition within it. They are personal in that they arise from one man's experience, both as an exile who has put down new roots, and as an individual who has had to find his own way to wisdom, renunciation and peace. The poems, I think, are informed by a sense of beauty and sadness, but they also speak of a lively and generous spirit, of a man with the gift of friendship.

Poetry is the most succinct and the most personal of the arts. The poet invites the reader into his own private world, the world of his own suffering and deepest feelings. But we are welcome only if we make the effort to comprehend. It is an effort well rewarded, and I am delighted that Emil Rado's poems are now available to a wide audience through their publication in this edition. I warmly commend them.

A VIEW FROM THE TRAIN

Setting off south from Glasgow, in brilliant, plangent light;
the sun, low in the sky, floodlights the Southern Uplands.
They look freshly carved:
the sculptor's chisel only just removed.
The smooth, massive hills seem strangely human;
sweeping, powerful limbs
curled in postures of guarded repose
as if protecting some tender secret.
Then, as the train swings round,
their inner structure is revealed:
a cleft in the ridge, a waterfall
flanked by a lush growth of trees.
Above, the drystane dykes
affirm the shape of the hills;
in the valleys, the grass glows unbelievably green
as if the light came from within.
Dykes, mounds and sprouting, ploughed furrows
cast deep shadows on the stroking-smooth grass.

Cattle surround a circular hay-feed,
Neatly aligned, like spokes of a wheel.

I close my eyes, to hold the vanishing moment;
Blow on the embers, fan them into flame.

November 1988

PARALLEL PATHS

Sailing from different harbours
bound for destinations we can only surmise,
our room for manoevre restricted by prior commitments;
our tracks run parallel, cross and re-cross,
yet never completely merge.
Twin souls, made for each other yet never entwined -
an occasion for grief or rejoicing, laughter or tears?

Who with a heart can fail to grieve
for glory glimpsed yet never attained?

But the future calls, rooted not in water but earth.

Let us make our crossings
verdant oases of our separate journeys,
where we can laugh or play,
nurture each other's strivings,
or tend one another's bruised souls.

July 1988

AUTUMN CLEAROUT

In the chill morning of early November
the plants in the porch longed for the warmth of August.
Time they were brought inside, I thought.

But the sun was bright, I had papers to read, so I turned on the heater and sat down among them;
we pretended it was still August.

The Cape primrose had had a splendid season,
in a profusion of flowers since May:
a flock of dancing blue butterflies.

Now they were wizened and dry, their colour all leached.
I laid them to rest
to dream of a Spring resurrection.

One flower remained, floating defiantly blue
on its still erect wiry stem,
flaunting its fugitive beauty.

That midsummer love was my last flower
I have plucked it and pressed it for you.

December 1988

A BRIEF ENCOUNTER

So there we sat at the end of the stalls,
I with a party of friends, you on your own.
On the stage, Fledermaus, a Christmas romp,
high spirits, backchat, pure Glasgow fun.

I turned to you, smiling, to share the enjoyment,
you smiled back relieved, no longer alone.
We exchanged no word, only smiles -
yet what a range of emotions smiles can express!

Tentative tendrils of transient love -
no hurt if it's fled;
Its magic's still held,
etched in our memory, safe in our head.

December 1988

ASSOCIATIONS

Gleaming, rich slices of freshly ploughed earth;
Spiders' webs glistening with fresh-fallen dew,
Enticing scent of newly baked bread -
The life-giving freshness of you.

February 1989

SERPENTINE IN A SIGNET RING

Glowing red veins in deep olive stone,
clasped in fine-crafted fingers of gold:
imprisoned or enhanced?

Here I am, back in England;
card in hand I stand by the phone,
wanting to call you -

yet I desist.
Is setting close limits on what we may do
the golden clasp
that guards the fine-cut jewel of our love?

April 1989

THE EBBING TIDE

Now that our friendship appears at an end,
Must we view past gladness through the cracked glass of pain?

Because you no longer seem to want to meet me,
was it less sweet
to have stood atop the jagged Ptarmachan
and watched clouds
racing their shadows below?
or floated, side by side, in velvet Abies Loch
one scorching summer day?

We have untied the knot
that moored the sturdy vessel of our friendship,
and let it float out of sight
on the fast-ebbing tide.

Row it back, if the tide ever turns...

April 1989

INCHCAILLOCH

There were rowing boats, sailing boats riding at anchor,
cygnets and swans coursed the sun-drenched bay;
gaily and strongly we cut through the water
as we swam to the island that far summer day.

* * *

It's a shimmer, a haze, now, an ocean of bluebells,
Down in the blue mist, hidden from view,
I drink in the beauty of new leaf on old tree,
As I lie on the warm earth, thinking of you.

May 1989

THOUGHTS IN BRODICK CASTLE

There was a stove in the castle bedroom,
just like the one in my grandfather's house:
yellow and blue Italian tiles, with curlicue markings,
that reached to the ceiling.
I warmed my hands on them, coming in from the snow,
while inside the fire soared...

I have built you a stove round my love,
to warm you but not to burn.

November 1989

NOVEMBER RUN

Seven o'clock drizzle
on a bleary November morning.
Below, in the park, mist,
transfixed by winter-bare beeches.
We set off,
prancing colts, shaking off shackles of night;
Glide on air,
as feet strike earth in soundless unison.
squirrel scuttles up tree;
a party of chattering magpies
land and swiftly depart:

Seven for the secret that never was told.

But we both know the secret...

November 1989

A COPPICED FRIENDSHIP

That proud beech is cut down to a stump,
the bird-song stilled in its branches.
It had grown too tall;
its roots could not hold it in such shallow soil.

Yet the sap still runs in the stump,
and buds are ready to burst on its new-born branches.

I tend it with watchful affection - and secateurs.

February 1990

SOARING WITH THE LARK

Do I diminish
    the rising lark's trill
By striving to grasp
    its unfading power to thrill?

We are brothers under the skin,
    he of the daring wing,
        I of the plodding step;
Poised on our hard-won peaks,
Intoxicated as we range
    over rivers that reach to oceans.

Being with you,
    I soar with the lark,
My wings paint shadows
    on the tilting horizon.

June 1990

FOCUSING

Have you noticed how,
when you focus a lens
On a malachite kingfisher
or a tiger orchid,
You see it
as you never see with the naked eye?
Every hair of its feather,
each incandescent blue,
distinct, pin sharp;
each curling petal
shaped by the hand
of the divine carver.
Everything else - only a blurred context,
a setting for a jewel of creation.

True love has eyes like a lens:
sees you as God will see you
on the day of judgement -
irreplaceable, unique.

I have no need to possess you,
barely even to touch you,
I just look at you
and give thanks you are there.

July 1990

LIKE ADAM

Can it be that we first met only yesterday?
Who are you, kindred soul, dreamer of my dreams?
My long lost friend, my sister or my love?
I hardly know; only that yesterday
your fingers touched my arm,
and I stood, rooted,
like Adam when he first set eyes on Eve,
and knew, and knew that from this day
our lives are interleaved.

September 1990

MINT ÁDÁM

Lehet, hogy tegnap még nem ismertelek?
S ma minden sejtemmel tudom, hogy egy vérből vagyunk.
Testvérem vagy? Leányom? Nagy szerelmem?
Ezt még nem tudom; csak azt,
Hogy mikor kezed karomba tetted,
Úgy álltam ott, mint Ádám,
Mikor Évát először látta meg;
És azt, hogy mától kezdve
Közünk van egymás életéhez.

Hungarian version *1990 szept*

TRUMPETS OF JOSHUA

Mid-January. Four o'clock. Light fades
on Possil's grim, half-deserted streets.
The morning joy of untouched white forgotten,
as tyres spin and squelch through grimy snow.

I turn to your cassette, and hear
full-throated song of nightingale and thrush,
robin and rising lark:
Trumpets of Joshua - they crack the walls of winter!

You slipped into my life
like summer birdsong into winter night -

sing on and stay for a while...

January, 1991

JÓZSUÉ HARSONÁI

Január vége felé jár. Alkonyodik
Glasgow elhagyatott, mord utcái felett.
Elfeledett már a bársonyos reggeli hó,
csúszik az abroncs a mocskos esteli sárban.

Lejátszom a te pesti kazettád, s hallom
fülemülék s pacsirták mámoros dalait:
Józsué harsonái - széjjelrepesztik a tél falait!

Úgy röppentél te az én életembe,
mint nyári madárdal a zord téli estbe -

Maradj még kicsit. Énekelj tovább...

Hungarian version *1991 január*

FREE SPIRIT

In memoriam E.L.T.

There was the train, hurtling ever southwards,
and all around us the mist.
Here and there one could just make out
a nestling, whitewashed farm,
With a battered car, tractor, scraggy ducks . . .
But the sheep melted into the fields,
and even the smallest hill disappeared out of sight,
almost before it got going.

Then I had this sense you were watching me:
I felt you were there, floating, dipping,
keeping pace with the train.
At peace. Having the time of your life.

Just like you, I thought.
Here we are, on our way to your funeral,
and you refusing to lie down in the box:
plunging into the mist, skimming over the hedge,
Overtaking the train -
A free spirit. Irrepressible. Unconfined.

I could swear I saw you wink at me once.

January 1991

ON FIDDEN BEACH

Perched on a ledge
I watch the rising tide
kiss and suck at red granite rocks below,
splintering shafts of sunlight.
The tide turns -
ringed plovers scuttle and skate
on the emerging sands,
as if blown by the wind.
Oystercatchers in full sartorial splendour
strut through reflected clouds
on the mirroring sands,
flashing beaks probing the depths.

Was it on such a day that,
His strenuous task accomplished,
He rested, and saw that it was good?

Illustration by Anne Rado, done while the poem was being written. July 1991

MEETING AND PARTING

In memory of Agi Blacklocks

The warm September sun drew us to Hampstead.
So long since we had met - so much to say
where should we start?
Yet, sitting by Highgate Pond
there was no need for words.
Content with being together,
we sat on the bench,
as golden showers of lime leaves
scattered and spun down the pond;
and the cream and russet reflections
of the Georgian houses
shivered when touched by the leaves,
then returned to stillness.

* * *

The old Armenian woman
won her fight with the slope
and shedding her basket and cares
sat down on our bench.
She needed our company more than the rest -
her family scattered, she unburdened her soul,
and for those fleeting moments
she belonged to our circle.

* * *

"Next spring we'll meet in Scotland", we parted.
And today, as the train sweeps me to Oban,
the trees are still in the myriad greens
of their midsummer garments.
A white mare steps in her field
as if bent on a mission;
and the first dusting of snow
coats Cruachan's massive shoulders.

* * *

If we had known we were parting for ever,
had I a gift for you
to lighten your longest journey?
Only this verse, and the sense of peace
at our meeting and parting.

September 1991

HOSPITAL THOUGHTS

from The Western Infirmary, Glasgow

Another long night's over.
From my high window
I watch tongues of sunlight
creep down the weathered gable ends,
pick out the distant cranes -
giant praying mantises, poised for attack.
Rows of red sandstone tenements
topped by cream chimney pots
spring into blazing life.
The first train snakes by...

We, too, crawl back to life.
Gingerly stretch our limbs,
get in touch with our pain,
swallow our pills, our cornflakes.
The consultant calls,
talks of histology tests,
a few days still to wait -
and the future clouds over
like a crazed windscreen.

In the next ward,
four ancient mariners,
years of cancer between them,
face it with disrespect and
flippant defiance;
talk of football, burst into raucous song.
And I join them - I, too, belong to Glasgow.

October 1991

ELEGY

Frosted crowns of hornbeam and oak
cast patterns on the dark winter sky.
They stand scattered, like souls of dead soldiers
returning to fields of lost battles . . .
The train gathers speed, and in the thickening mist
I search for your voice, your walk -
the voice unexpectedly deep, the walk jaunty and gay,
and that jubilant face
comprehending the world for the first time,
eager for fresh miracles.

Watching you then, full of promise and beauty,
who could foresee the road
that led to that lonely room -
in your body the needle of death,
in your womb a child not to be born?

What forces destroyed you?
Was the seed fatally flawed, or the soil too stony?

Your death leaves me diminished,
Colours for ever robbed from my rainbow.

December, 1991

KILCHATTAN BAY

Gingerly picking our way by the shore,
an eye on the menacing clouds,
we watch sunlit waves
lazily sweep, gather, then explode
on the resilient rock,
scattering diamond spray.

jutting red sandstone slabs
- tattered battle-flags -
show marks of the ceaseless struggle:
now densely carved, like a brain,
now all delicate tracery.

Redshanks and turnstones
quarter the pebbly shore,
and the breeze that ruffles the sea
barely disturbs the flocks of chestnut-bright wigeon
or the harlequin rafts of eiders plaintively cooing.

We round the point and
trudge up the ridge
to find a green dream-world
of frozen volcanic sea;
we climb crest after soaring crest,
laugh as we lean on the gale,
survey our distant domains,
almost float with the gulls -

then, hand in hand,
we slowly descend
the precipitous slope to Kilchattan.

January 1992

FLOWERS OF WINTER

A winter morning's walk,
myself still shaky, just out of hospital,
surmising death,
you still in the grip of bereavement.
We had both walked that moor before,
but not this particular path;
now, in the mist that almost concealed you
as you walked by my side
it looked new -
full of unrevealed promise.

At the crest of a slope,
suddenly the mist was below us,
and we stood in a meadow -
dense with sparkling white flowers?
I knelt down to grasp this midwinter miracle:
seed-heads of grass,
long relieved of their load,
their empty seed-stalks
bent with a million dew drops,
each one reflecting the sun.

And the shadows of death dispersed
like the mist in the rising sun.

January 1992

WHEN I THINK OF YOU

When I think of you -
I see larches,
their fresh green glowing
in the late winter sun.
I hear soft summer breezes
scamper through poppy-strewn cornfields,
and brooks, telling their tales
of faraway uplands.
An otter floats in her pool,
crunching a freshly caught eel . . .

. . .and I marvel how,
after so much suffering,
you still radiate sparkle and peace.

February 1992

GODDESS ON THE 5.35

Paddington:
the 5.35 is packed to the gunwales;
the strains of a weary day
only partly eased by the homeword journey.
We sit,
our anxieties etched in our faces,
or stir in uneasy sleep -
'seconds' from Heaven's winter sales.

And there she was
on the opposite bench:
serene,
with her ebony velvet skin,
fearless, dancing eyes
smiling a secret smile;
her delicate nose
so exactly placed
above the fine-chiselled lips.

And I wondered -
is she aware
that alongside her
the rest of us all seem
children of a lesser God?

And if not,
would she like to be told?

I never found out:
she got off at Ealing Broadway.

February 1992

ALMOST A HAIKU

You don't even

need to speak:

You just walk

through the door -

and I can hear

the music

of the spheres.

March 1992

TERMS OF ENDEARMENT

To my wife

I hold you close in my arms, and
as I caress you,
my words seek to echo my hands -
How confined are our thoughts by language!
I search through terms of endearment, and
find no expressions to say
"I don't own you", that
"I love your wild sense of freedom;
your zest for adventure,
your feel for where lies true north."

No one can own you . . .

As I wake every morning,
my hands reach out to find you, and I
give thanks that you're still choosing
to take this journey with me.

March 1992

SZERELMES SZAVAK

Feleségemnek

Karomban tartalak,
és amig ölellek,
szavaim visszhangozzák kezem -
Milyen korlátoló a nyelv!
Kutatom a szerelem szótárát,
s nincs rá kifejezés, hogy:
"nem vagy tulajdonom",
"szabad vagy mint egy madár",
"szeretem nyiltságod minden újra,
s azt, hogy mindig tudod,
hová vezet az út".

Tulajdona nem lehetsz senkinek . . .

Reggel, ha ébredek,
téged keres kezem,
és áldom sorsomat,
hogy ezen az uton együtt jössz velem.

Hungarian version *1992 március*

WHAT LIES IN STORE FOR YOU?

We sat side by side on the train,
you a twelve year old child,
I an elderly man;
I watched the careless grace of your movements,
your face so exquisitely carved, and
that wicked grin of complicity
as our eyes met . . .
So disturbingly like that other young woman
I had loved as a child,
who died by the needle of death.

What lies in store for you? I wondered;
could I protect you
if I told you how she had rebelled,
and destroyed only herself?
But I stayed silent:
how could a fleeting acquaintance
impart so momentous a message?

May guardian angels watch over you, and
help you foresee where your chosen path leads.

April 1992

THE HARP ROCK

Half submerged by the sea,
your stout frame still intact,
defying fierce seas and winter gales;
but your strings are away,
their music forever stilled -
a blind harp, left by a blind harper.

Did you watch, long ago,
when the landlords' men
drove their own huddled kin
to this desolate shore
to start a new life
on a thin strip of land
with nothing but seaweed and sand?
Was it their bitter tears
broke your heart and strangled your music?

Today the summer sky is
dizzy with lark song,
and purposeful bees feast on seapink and clover;
a few tourists stroll by
to savour the peace of the scene . . .
Only I,
a piece of living Holocaust driftwood,
strain to decipher the song of the harp.

July 1992

Some of the harshest incidents of the Highland Clearances occurred on the Moray coast. Just off this shore, at Portknockie, lies an amazingly harp-like sea-stack, to which the title refers.

LOOKING AT OLD PHOTOGRAPHS

Working steadily,
clearing my room for the painter,
I was quite unprepared for my feelings
when I opened that brown envelope.
Never quite forgot it was there,
nor the late summer day
when we strolled to that wood -
finding a remote, sunny clearing,
I tried to capture
not just your heart-stopping beauty,
but the tenderness we felt for each other.
How well I succeeded! So many years ago -
it feels like a lifetime...

Why did I never look at them again?
Perhaps, like needing to watch an eclipse
through darkened glass,
it felt safer to recall you
through the filter of memories;
maybe in later years
I could not face the pain
of seeing in print the love that had fled.

Looking back, now that both of our hearts are
at peace with our loyalties,
how do I think of that friendship?
Was it a reckless mistake? Did the pains of our parting
eclipse the joy that we gave and received?
I often wonder...
Yet, now that the sands of my life
are running their last through the hour-glass,
and the shadow of death is my constant companion,
I still remember
that brief blaze of unfettered glory;
and give thanks for the fire
that we stole from the gods.

August 1992

THE MUSHROOM FEAST

Walking through autumn woods
in dappled sunshine,
path barely visible
under drifts of chestnut and lime leaves.
Twigs snap and beetles scatter
as our eyes tune in
to a profusion of mushrooms.
Their anonymous menace soon resolves
into familiar faces:
succulent clumps of gold honey fungus,
furled white umbrellas of shaggy ink-caps,
ungainly grace of glazed penny buns,
treacherous lure of the red amanita.

With deft strokes of the knife
our baskets fill as our appetites mount;
the beckoning pleasures
of a rich autumn feast
spiced
by knowing we've safely walked
where many would fear to tread.

September 1992

CANOEING ON HAMBURG'S CANALS

for Anne

A small canoe
glides on the narrow canal,
its prow gently splits
glowing reflections
of sunlit trees with their leaves on fire -
willows and limes and tall Spanish chestnuts
edging the gardens
of handsome white villas.
In the light breeze
their curled up leaves
float alongside us:
a tiny flotilla, marking our progress.
Our paddles rise and fall,
raise a cascade of spray,
while our boat ploughs a straight furrow
towards a distant pool and
a pair of great crested grebes.
Now the water is all burnished gold,
and the slanting sunlight
catches your hair, your crimson blouse,
your paddle poised to descend -

- and I hold fast to the peace of that moment,
to be my *mantra*,
when the long white fingers of death
reach out to take me away.

November 1992

The urge to capture moments of great happiness and to hold on to them for later use is one of the strongest human drives. In my own predicament, trying to come to terms with the sense of approaching death, I have tried to summon up the image of a moment of supreme happiness, not as a shield against death, but to pave, so to speak, a safe passage from the here to the hereafter.

Three Prose Poems

A NIGHT STROLL ON THE WYE

One of the underrated pleasures of life is walking out of doors in seemingly total darkness, and finding the eye rapidly adjusting; seeing not only movement and shape, but even colour and texture. The other night I found myself walking through the meadows in Bakewell, where the Wye runs in large lazy loops that almost touch. Normally a slow-moving river hereabouts, now it was in spate, moving faster than walking pace.

As my eye adjusted to the dark, I noticed a mallard drake tailing and courting a white farmyard duck. When the moon rose clear of the clouds, the ducks' shadows sat sharp on the water. They were moving at a good speed against the current, when suddenly both turned and, pointing downstream, started to feed, yet remaining stationary in midcurrent.

How did they manage to stay still facing downstream, unless they had double-jointed feet? It puzzled me, until I had a chance to return to the spot by daylight. At the point where the ducks had turned, the stream was parted by a large submerged rock, the arms of the current reuniting a yard or two further downstream. Between these arms lay a small island of still water, where ducks could safely graze. Their stillness in that rushing river brought to my mind pelicans I used to watch in Kenya, their wings motionless, yet spiralling ever higher on invisible thermal currents, seeming to defy gravity.

April 1987

ABOUT EIDERS AND GORSE

It is strange how, for years, we may fail to notice what our eyes can see and our ears can hear. Then one day they stand up and almost grab us by the throat. I think in the years to come I shall remember this sodden spring of 1992 with its occasional days of brilliance, for my discovery of the sound of eiders and the scent of the gorse.

I have been a casual bird-watcher along the shores of Scotland for a good slice of my life, but never before have I noticed that eiders made a sound. Then last spring my wife came back from a weekend's camping on Bute and told me of this strange sound she heard all night, in between the wild, exultant cackle of the oystercatchers and the melodious trills of the curlew. "I think it may have been the eiders" she said, "but with so many other birds around, I couldn't be sure. It was a strange *Aw-wooo!* sound, that I would have taken for a distant calf rather than a bird, but there it was, drifting across the water."

Last weekend we were back on Bute, walking in Kilchattan Bay, and this time there could be no doubt about it. Rafts of harlequin eiders were everywhere, and the plaintive sound of *Aw-wooo! Aw-wooo!* echoed all along the shore. The sound seemed to come from the males (both those accompanied by females and those on their own). A fetching "invitation to the waltz", probably - but how did we manage not to hear it all these years?

My other discovery was the scent of the gorse. A few weeks ago my wife and I were taking that prince of Galloway shore-walks, from Sandyhills to Rockcliffe, in the company of a friend. All night and all morning the wind had howled and the rain fell in sheets, then at lunch-time both wind and rain left us abruptly, to go and trouble the English, and we were granted an afternoon of almost Hebridean clarity. "Can you smell the gorse?" our friend asked, as we threaded our way along paths banked by blazing gold. Only politeness stopped us replying "don't be silly, we've been walking among gorse all our adult lives: gorse has no scent." But we were wrong: as we gingerly approached the bushes, the lips of the flowers wide-open in the warm sun, we were astonished by their intense coconut scent.

On a dull day or in half-shade, the florets are closed and give out no scent.But the other day, walking in brilliant sunshine on Bute, among the sweeping hills among Kilchattan, our noses now "tuned in", every fresh breeze was laden with the intoxicating coconut scent of the nearby fields of Gorse.

May 1992

ROOTS THAT SHATTER AND BIND

It must be almost twenty years ago that I first noticed that birch, growing straight out of a boulder on Rannoch Moor, on the way to Glencoe. The rock was a massive piece of granite, the size of a small house; the birch a mere sapling: a foot or two, no more. There must have been a pocket of soil where the seed had landed - I thought - but it won't get far.

Since then, I have often driven past that rock. Against all the odds, the birch has survived; not just living, but thriving. When I last saw it a short while ago, it was over ten feet tall; in the late afternoon sun it was like a green flame issuing from a silver torch.

How could it have grown so tall - I wondered - with so little to sustain it? The answer lay in the roots. The slow, surging force of their growth had split the rock, allowing the wind to blow earth into the fissures, while other roots grew over the rock, binding the riven boulder together.

The striking image of that birch growing out of the boulder, shattering it, yet holding it together, has kept returning to me ever since. I knew it had a meaning, but the meaning kept eluding me. Then last Sunday, in the silence of a Quaker Meeting, it came to me. God has a purpose for each one of us, and that purpose takes root in us, like the birch in the rock, whether we will it or no. If we permit it to grow, it takes over our life, breaking it up, yet binding it together. It consumes us, until there is no telling which is the birch and which is the rock.

August 1990